new her chocolate
cake, fudge brownies,
chocolate-banana pie,
chocolates, mint julep
ke pudding, chocolate
colate caramels, triple-
olate mousse parfaits,
e truffle pie, chocolate
te-peanut butter balls,
nocolate meringue pie,

Forrest's Fudge Cake, page 24

Groovy Grasshopper Pie, page 99

"Life is like a box of chocolates"

Forrest Gump™

MY FAVORITE

Chocolate Recipes

Mama's fudge, cookies, cakes, and candies

Oxmoor House®

This is a Time Inc. Ventures Custom Publishing Book.

Recipes and food photography
©1995 Oxmoor House, Inc.

FORREST GUMP™ & ©1995 Paramount Pictures.
All rights reserved.
Oxmoor House Authorized User.

Introductions ©1995 Winston Groom

Library of Congress Catalog Card Number: 95-67293
ISBN: 0-8487-1487-3

Printed in the U.S.A.
First Printing 1995

Cover inset photo: Forrest's Fudge Cake, page 24, Chocolate-Mint
Truffles, page 54, 'Bama Bittersweet Truffles, page 53,
Chunky Hazelnut-Toffee Cookies, page 72

To order more copies of FORREST GUMP: MY FAVORITE CHOCOLATE
RECIPES or to order THE BUBBA GUMP SHRIMP CO. COOKBOOK,
write to Oxmoor House, P.O. Box 2463, Birmingham, AL 35201

4

ontents

Dedicated to my Mama,
who's makin' heaven a better place.

Dear Chocolate Lovers,

 Let me say this: Besides my Mama's shrimp, the best things in my life was her chocolates! Why, when I was little, I once even imagined her fixin' chocolate-covered shrimp! Now Mama, she didn't think that was such a good idea, but what she done the next day was to make me some chocolate candy in the shape of shrimps, an' that was sure good enough for me.

 I want to tell you how I feel about chocolate in this book, an' that's tough. It's like tryin' to explain blue to a beagle—know what I mean? So maybe I'll just talk a little about Mama.

 Now Mama was good in the kitchen; ain't no doubt about that. We had one of them big ol' range stoves an' when I'd come home from school every afternoon, I can just see her now workin' over that stove on somethin', an' whatever it was, you could smell it all the way down the street. But my favorite times was when I could smell her fixin' chocolate, 'cause I knew I was gonna get to lick the spoon!

 Whether it was cakes or candy or fudge or anythin', Mama would start with a big ol' iron pot over the fire. An' then she'd throw in a big ol' block of brown chocolate stuff an' put in a little cream an' always add a little extra sugar, just for me. An' after awhile, the stuff be bubblin' an' steamin' an' Mama'd be stirrin' an' talkin' at the same time. An' after awhile, she'd turn off the stove an' keep on stirrin' an' I'd ask her when I was gonna get to lick the spoon, an' she'd always say, "Just wait a few minutes, Forrest, it ain't cool enough yet." An' that was always my least favorite part.

Finally the time would come, an' she'd take that big ol' wood spoon an' give the chocolate another stir or two, an' tho' she never said it, I know she'd scoop up a little more chocolate, just for me. An' then she'd hand me the spoon an' I'd lick it clean!

After that, she'd spread that chocolate over a big ol' cake she had goin' in the oven, or she'd spoon it out into little tin shapes that she had sittin' on wax paper, or pour it over a pan of brownies—an' I knew I was gonna get to eat it again right after supper.

Now let me tell you, I've eaten some store-bought chocolates in my time, but wadn't nothin' better than Mama's. An' I bet when you use this cookbook, if you use it just the way it tells you to, you'll be sayin' the same thing.

YOURS TRULY,
FORREST GUMP

8

"Life is like a box of chocolates"

About Chocolate

Now they says chocolate was invented by Mexican Indians 'bout a thousand years ago. This was news to me. I thought Mama invented it. But anyways, the explorers from Spain came an' stole all the Indians' chocolate recipes (an' everythin' else, while they was at it), an' so chocolate done took the Old World by storm! People ate it, drank it, took it for medicine, an' even used it for money.

All of this should come as no big surprise, seein' how good chocolate is. It's sweet (mostly), it tastes good, an' you feel good after you've eaten some. But remember, it's not smart to eat somethin' like two or three pounds of it at a time, or, like Mama always says, you'll wind up feelin' green 'round the gills, whatever that means.

9

ALL CHOCOLATES IS NOT ALIKE

I thought chocolates was chocolates until one day when I finished off a box of chocolates an' I still wanted more. It was then I learnt that all chocolates is not alike. See, I knowed where Mama kept her cookin' chocolate so I snitched one of them little squares that she melts down an' puts in her pies. It looked an' felt like chocolate, so I took a big ol' bite an' soon as I did, I let out such a gasp that Mama came runnin'. Not only was I caught red-handed, but that stuff was the worst stuff I ever tasted. I thought it was spoilt or something an' that I'd get in big trouble on top of that, but I didn't. Mama couldn't stop laughin'. Finally she said, "Forrest, that's not the kind of chocolate you eat! It doesn't have any sugar in it!"

Well, anyways, Mama sat down an' 'splained 'bout all the kinds of chocolate there is. It all seems pretty complicated, but Mama says it's not. An' she says the SOUTHERN LIVIN' recipes always tells you exactly what you need an' you just go to the store an' get it. Anyways, I never wanted to be confused again 'bout what kind of chocolate is fer eatin' so Mama wrote down these notes to help me keep it straight. Mama was a real smart lady.

Unsweetened Chocolate: Used for cooking and not eating, Forrest, unsweetened chocolate is pure and simple chocolate liquor, the base other chocolates are made from. Candymakers don't add sugar or flavoring; they just shape it into 1-ounce blocks and sell it in 8-ounce packages.

Semisweet Chocolate: When they add sugar, extra cocoa butter, and flavorings to unsweetened chocolate, they call it semisweet chocolate, Forrest. They mold the dark chocolate into 1-ounce blocks or into morsels, which are chips specially made to hold their shape softly when baked, like in those chocolate chip cookies I make you, honey. If the package says "chocolate flavored," it's not the real thing, but a chocolate substitute made from vegetable oil and cocoa rather than unsweetened chocolate and cocoa butter. Semisweet chocolate is made for cooking, but it's OK for nibblin', too.

Sweet Baking Chocolate: Sometimes called German's sweet chocolate after the man who first made it, this chocolate is similar to the semisweet kind but it has more sugar. You'd like it for nibblin', too! It comes in 4-ounce bars.

Milk Chocolate: Milder and sweeter than semisweet chocolate, this kind has milk or cream added to the chocolate liquor, cocoa butter, and sugar. It's usually used for eating, Forrest, but you can cook with it, if you don't turn the heat up too high.

Cocoa: This is a highly concentrated kind of chocolate they make by taking most of the cocoa butter out of the chocolate liquor. Then they grind the liquor that's left into a fine powder. They don't add sugar or flavoring, and cocoa has the least fat of any real chocolate. It's easy to use because you don't have to melt it.

Chocolate Syrup: A combination of cocoa, corn syrup, and flavoring, chocolate syrup comes in jars, cans, or plastic containers. This is what you like to squeeze into your milk and lick from a spoon, Forrest.

Chocolate-Flavored Candy Coating: Sometimes called candy coating, almond bark, or compound coatings, this is made from vegetable fat instead of cocoa butter, and has coloring and flavoring added. It's not considered real chocolate because it doesn't have chocolate liquor or cocoa butter. It's sold in blocks and discs, and a lot of times it comes in pretty colors and nice fruit flavors. I sometimes use it when I'm going to dip chocolates because it has a high melting point (that means it doesn't burn as easily as real chocolate) and it firms back up after it's melted and won't stick to your fingers like real chocolate sometimes does, if you don't temper it. (I'll tell you about tempering later, Forrest.)

White Chocolate: This is also not real chocolate because it doesn't have any chocolate liquor but, unlike the candy coating I told you about, it does have cocoa butter in it. That gives it a nice aroma and a texture more like real chocolate—more so than that candy coating has, anyway. The two products often cook up differently in recipes, so read your labels carefully, Forrest, to see whether or not the stuff has cocoa butter.

Thanks, Mama ...

for explainin' things so's I could always understand.

SUBSTITUTIN' CHOCOLATE

Yep, I learnt the hard way that all chocolate's not alike, but Mama says sometimes you can swap one type for another when you're cookin', if you don't have just what the recipe calls for. She drew up this chart to help me keep 'em straight.

Chocolate Substitution Chart

To substitute for:	Use:
1 (1-ounce) square unsweetened chocolate	• 3 tablespoons cocoa plus 1 tablespoon shortening
1 ounce semisweet chocolate	• 1 ounce (about 3 tablespoons) semisweet chocolate morsels • 1 (1-ounce) square unsweetened chocolate plus 1 tablespoon sugar • 1 ounce sweet baking chocolate
6-ounce package (1 cup) semisweet chocolate morsels	• 6 tablespoons cocoa, ⅓ cup sugar, plus ¼ cup shortening • 2 ounces unsweetened chocolate, 2 tablespoons shortening, plus ½ cup sugar
4-ounce bar sweet baking chocolate	• ¼ cup cocoa, ⅓ cup sugar, plus 3 tablespoons shortening

STORIN' CHOCOLATE

Like I said, Mama kept her cookin' chocolates in the cupboard, but after she caught me snitchin' 'em, she put 'em someplace else. Then I couldn't find 'em, but here's what she wrote down fer me 'bout where I should store mine.

Chocolate stays fresh a year or more if well wrapped and stored in a cool, dry place (65° to 70°). Sometimes it turns a misty-gray color, but that doesn't mean it's spoiled. They call this a "bloom"; it means that the chocolate got too hot or too humid. Don't worry about bloom; it doesn't affect flavor or quality.

MELTIN' CHOCOLATE

I knows one surefire way to melt chocolate. Ya see, one day I was gonna surprise Jenny with some chocolate. So I grabbed three pieces of that kind with the nuts an' I hid 'em in my pocket. An' Jenny an' I was talkin' up in our tree, an' when the time was right, I pulled 'em out, but the wrappin's was 'bout all that was left 'cause they'd all run together. She said it was sweet of me anyways to bring 'em. Mama got my pants clean OK. She said next time just take her a box of chocolate rather than hidin' it an' all. An' when I really wanted to melt chocolates, here's what she said:

Always melt chocolate using real low heat, Forrest, because it burns easily. If you try to melt it in a regular pan, you'll burn it for sure. I always use my double boiler, and I've heard you can do it in one of those new microwave ovens.

Make sure the container you melt it in is real dry because the tiniest little bit of water can make it clump all up faster than you can run. And if you've got a big chunk of chocolate, chop it up first to help it melt more evenly.

There's one tricky part, honey. If you're melting sweet or semisweet chocolate, it's gonna pretty much stay in its shape until you stir it a little to help it along. If you just keep cooking and waiting for it to melt down and get flat, you'll burn it. Just stir it as you go, and it'll be all right.

If you're using a double boiler, put the chocolate in the top and melt it over hot, but not boiling, water. Don't cover it. And don't forget to stir. If you get one of those microwaves, here's a little chart I found that should help.

Microwave Melting Chart			
Chocolate	Amount	Power	Minutes
Morsels	½ to 1 cup	MEDIUM	2 to 3
	1½ cups	MEDIUM	3 to 3½
	2 cups	MEDIUM	3½ to 4
Squares	1 to 2 squares	MEDIUM	1½ to 2
	3 squares	MEDIUM	2
	4 to 5 squares	MEDIUM	2 to 2½
	6 squares	MEDIUM	2½ to 3

Place chocolate in a 1-quart glass bowl; microwave at MEDIUM (50% power) until melted, stirring once.

GARNISHIN' WITH CHOCOLATE

*Mama said chocolate curls are real neat when you're tryin'
to do somethin' nice, so she wrote about fancy stuff, too.*

Chocolate Leaves: Use nonpoisonous leaves like mint
or rose leaves. Wash and pat dry. Melt 1 or 2 (1-ounce)
squares of semisweet chocolate over hot water in a double
boiler; let chocolate cool slightly. Using a knife, spread a
thin layer of chocolate on the back of each leaf. Place on a
wax paper-lined baking sheet, chocolate side up; freeze
until chocolate is firm, about 10 minutes. Grasp the leaf at
the stem end, and gently peel away from the chocolate.

Chocolate Curls: Melt 4 (1-ounce) squares of semisweet
chocolate over hot water in a double boiler. Pour it onto a
wax paper-lined baking sheet. Spread it into a 3-inch-wide
strip. Smooth top with a spatula. Chill until it feels slightly
tacky but not firm. (If it's too hard, Forrest, the curls will
break; if too soft, the chocolate won't curl.) Gently pull a
vegetable peeler across the chocolate until curls form.
Transfer curls by inserting a wooden pick inside them.

Grated Chocolate: Use a hand grater or food processor
on any kind of chocolate to make fancy dessert sprinkles.

Chocolate Shavings: Gently pull a vegetable peeler
down one edge of a milk chocolate candy bar, letting the
chocolate curl up and drop into shavings.

MOLDIN' CANDIES LIKE IN A BOX OF CHOCOLATES

You know by now that I think my Mama could do 'bout anythin' she set her mind to. She could even make those pretty little chocolates like comes in the store-bought boxes—the ones that are molded in the pretty shapes an' sometimes there's surprises hidin' inside. An' 'cause Mama's always believed I could do anythin' I wanted, she set down those directions for me, too.

Thanks, Mama...

for settin' down all this stuff about chocolate for me.

Now, Forrest, you can make those fancy chocolates you love so much just by melting regular semisweet chocolate and spooning it into the little plastic molds like the recipes on pages 40 through 46 tell you to. But the real candy-makers have a little trick called tempering the chocolate that's probably what makes you like their candy so much.

Tempering slowly raises, lowers, and raises again the temperature of melted chocolate. It's more complicated than melting chocolate for making cakes and pies, but it's worth the time it takes. Tempered chocolate has a smooth, shiny, professional look. It quickly dries to a crisp snap and won't melt on your fingers as easily as chocolate melted the regular way does. It's great when you're molding candies because it makes them pop out of the molds easily.

Each of my candy recipes calls for a certain amount of tempered chocolate, and several of them call for Royal Icing, too. Here're the recipes you'll need to make them, honey. And don't let anybody tell you that you can't do it.

Tempered Chocolate

Semisweet chocolate squares

Grate or chop amount of chocolate recipe calls for. Place two-thirds of chocolate in top of a double boiler. Heat over hot, not boiling, water, stirring constantly, until chocolate reaches 115°. Place top of boiler on a towel. Add remaining one-third of chocolate to that in boiler, stirring until melted.

Pour chocolate onto a marble or laminate surface. Using a spatula, scrape and stir chocolate to smooth and cool it. When cooled to 80° to 82°, return it to top of double boiler. Place over hot, not boiling, water; heat and stir constantly, until it reaches 87° to 91°. Remove top of double boiler, and use tempered chocolate for molding candies as recipe directs.

Thanks, Mama ...

for showin' me the value of a box of chocolates.

Royal Icing

3 tablespoons commercial meringue powder
¼ cup plus 2 tablespoons warm water
1 (16-ounce) package powdered sugar, sifted
Paste food coloring (optional)

Combine meringue powder and warm water in a large mixing bowl. Beat at medium speed with an electric mixer until frothy. Add half of powdered sugar, mixing well. Add remaining sugar, and beat at high speed 5 to 7 minutes. Color as desired with food coloring. Yield: 3 cups.

Assorted chocolate candies, pages 40 through 46

Mighty Nice Chocolate Pastry Cake, page 28

"Life is like a box of chocolates"

$\mathcal{C}$akes

At Mama's boardin' house, Sunday was always cake day. Most everybody'd be dressed up from church an' it was not only the boarders, but people would drive from miles around 'cause they knew they was gonna get Mama's chocolate cake for their dessert.

Now there was always a lot left over for me to take to school (Mama saw to that!), an' it was in the lunchroom where I discovered that everybody else's mamas didn't make chocolate cake good as Mama could. I figgered this out because the other kids was always throwin' their cake at each other; but me, I just sat there an' ate mine to the last crumb. Good ol' Mama.

Black "Forrest" Cake

2   cups sifted cake flour
2   cups sugar
¾   cup cocoa
1¼   teaspoons baking powder
¼   teaspoon baking soda
¾   teaspoon salt
½   cup shortening
½   cup sour cream, divided
½   cup milk
⅓   cup kirsch or other cherry-flavored brandy
2   large eggs
2   egg yolks
4   cups whipping cream
⅓   cup sifted powdered sugar
2   tablespoons kirsch or other cherry-flavored brandy
2   (21-ounce) cans cherry pie filling

Grease two 9-inch round cakepans; line bottoms with wax paper. Grease and flour wax paper and sides of pans.

Combine first 6 ingredients in a large mixing bowl. Add shortening and ¼ cup sour cream, and beat at low speed with an electric mixer 30 seconds or until dry ingredients are moistened. Add remaining ¼ cup sour cream, milk, and ⅓ cup kirsch. Beat at medium speed 1½ minutes. Add eggs and egg yolks, one at a time, beating mixture 20 seconds after each addition.

Pour batter into prepared pans. Bake at 350° for 30 to 35 minutes or until a wooden pick inserted in center comes out clean. Cool in pans on wire racks 10 minutes; remove from pans. Peel off wax paper, and cool cake layers on wire racks. Split cake layers in half horizontally to make 4 layers. Position knife blade in food processor bowl.

Break 1 cake layer into pieces; place in bowl, and pulse 5 or 6 times or until cake resembles fine crumbs. Set aside.

Beat whipping cream until foamy; gradually add powdered sugar, beating until soft peaks form. Add 2 tablespoons kirsch, beating until stiff peaks form. Reserve 1½ cups whipped cream to use as garnish.

Place 1 cake layer on cake plate; spread with 1 cup whipped cream, and top with 1 cup cherry pie filling. Repeat procedure once, and top with remaining cake layer. Frost top and sides of cake with whipped cream. Pat cake crumbs around sides of cake. Pipe or dollop reserved 1½ cups whipped cream around top edges of cake; spoon 1 cup pie filling in center. (Reserve any remaining pie filling for other uses.) Cover and chill 8 hours. Yield: one 3-layer cake.

Thanks, Mama ...

for teachin' me that God didn't intend everybody to be the same. If he did, he'd a given 'em all braces on their legs.

Forrest's Fudge Cake

⅓   cup water
2   (1-ounce) squares unsweetened chocolate
⅔   cup shortening
2¾   cups sugar, divided
2   large eggs
2½   cups all-purpose flour
1¾   teaspoons baking soda
¾   teaspoon salt, divided
1   cup buttermilk
1   tablespoon plus 1 teaspoon vanilla extract,
         divided
¼   cup all-purpose flour
1   cup milk
½   cup butter, softened
½   cup shortening
Creamy Chocolate Frosting
Garnish: chocolate curls

Thanks, Mama ...

*for always givin'
me the very last
piece of cake.*

Combine water and chocolate in a small heavy saucepan;
cook over low heat, stirring constantly, until chocolate melts.
Remove from heat; let cool.

Beat ⅔ cup shortening at medium speed with an electric mixer until creamy; gradually add 1¾ cups sugar, beating
well. Add eggs, one at a time; beat well after each addition.
Combine 2½ cups flour, soda, and ½ teaspoon salt; add to
shortening mixture alternately with buttermilk, beginning and
ending with flour mixture. Mix after each addition. Add
cooled chocolate and 1 teaspoon vanilla, and mix just until
blended.

Pour batter into 3 greased and floured 9-inch round
cakepans. Bake at 350° for 20 to 25 minutes or until a
wooden pick inserted in center comes out clean. Cool in pans

on wire racks 10 minutes; remove from pans, and let cool completely on wire racks.

Place ¼ cup flour in a small saucepan; gradually stir in milk. Cook over low heat, stirring constantly, until thick. Remove from heat; let cool completely.

Beat butter and ½ cup shortening at medium speed until creamy; gradually add remaining 1 cup sugar, beating well. Add remaining 1 tablespoon vanilla, remaining ¼ teaspoon salt, and flour mixture; beat until smooth. Spread filling between cake layers. Spread Creamy Chocolate Frosting on top and sides of cake. Garnish, if desired. Yield: one 3-layer cake.

Creamy Chocolate Frosting

3   cups sugar
¾   cup milk
¾   cup butter or margarine
3   (1-ounce) squares unsweetened chocolate
¾   teaspoon vanilla extract

Combine first 4 ingredients in a large saucepan; cook over low heat, stirring constantly, until chocolate melts. Cook over medium heat, stirring constantly, until mixture boils; boil 1 minute, stirring constantly. Remove from heat, and stir in vanilla. Beat at high speed with an electric mixer over ice water 5 minutes. Remove from ice water, and continue to beat until frosting is spreading consistency (about 20 to 30 minutes). Immediately spread on cake. Yield: enough for one 3-layer cake.

Lt. Dan's Truffle Cake

1	cup cocoa
2	cups boiling water
1	cup butter or margarine, softened
2½	cups sugar
4	large eggs
1½	teaspoons vanilla extract
2¾	cups all-purpose flour
2	teaspoons baking soda
½	teaspoon baking powder
½	teaspoon salt

Truffle Filling and Chocolate Truffles
Satiny Chocolate Frosting
½   cup chocolate sprinkles

Combine cocoa and boiling water, stirring until smooth. Set aside.

Beat butter and next 3 ingredients at high speed with an electric mixer until fluffy (about 5 minutes). Combine flour and next 3 ingredients; add to butter mixture alternately with cocoa mixture, beginning and ending with flour mixture. Mix at low speed after each addition until blended.

Pour batter into 3 greased and floured 9-inch cakepans. Bake at 350° for 25 to 30 minutes. Cool in pans on wire racks 10 minutes; remove from pans, and let cool completely on wire racks.

Spread 1¼ cups Truffle Filling between layers. Spoon about 1 cup Satiny Chocolate Frosting into a decorating bag fitted with a large star tip. Spread remaining frosting on top and sides of cake, smoothing with a long metal spatula. Pat chocolate sprinkles on sides of cake; pipe or dollop a ring of frosting around top edge of cake. Arrange truffles on frosting ring. Cover and chill at least 8 hours. Yield: one 3-layer cake.

Truffle Filling and Chocolate Truffles

1   (12-ounce) package semisweet chocolate morsels
⅓   cup butter or margarine, cut into pieces
⅓   cup sifted powdered sugar
1   tablespoon egg substitute
2   tablespoons milk
3   tablespoons chocolate sprinkles

Melt chocolate morsels in a saucepan over low heat, stirring often. Remove from heat. Gradually add butter and powdered sugar, beating at medium speed with an electric mixer until mixture is smooth. Add egg substitute, beating well.

Place ½ cup mixture in a small bowl; cover with a paper towel, and let stand in a cool, dry place 1 hour (do not refrigerate). Add milk to remaining mixture, beating at high speed until spreading consistency. Spread immediately between cake layers.

Shape remaining ½ cup mixture into 12 equal balls; roll lightly in sprinkles. Yield: 1¼ cups filling and 12 truffles.

Thanks, Mama …

for makin' our house somewhere I always wanted to come home to.

Satiny Chocolate Frosting

1   (6-ounce) package semisweet chocolate
       morsels
½   cup half-and-half
1   cup butter or margarine
2½ cups sifted powdered sugar

Combine first 3 ingredients in a large saucepan; cook over medium heat, stirring constantly, until chocolate melts and mixture is smooth. Remove from heat; stir in powdered sugar. Let stand 20 minutes.

Place pan in a bowl of ice water, and beat at medium speed with an electric mixer until spreading consistency. Yield: 3½ cups.

Mighty Nice Chocolate Pastry Cake

2   (4-ounce) packages sweet baking chocolate
½   cup sugar
½   cup water
1½ teaspoons instant coffee granules
2   teaspoons vanilla extract
1   (11-ounce) package piecrust mix
2   cups whipping cream
Garnish: chocolate curls

Thanks, Mama ...

for makin' me understand that nobody is better than me.

Combine first 4 ingredients in a heavy saucepan; cook over low heat, stirring constantly, until mixture is smooth. Stir in vanilla. Cool mixture to room temperature.

Combine piecrust mix and ¾ cup chocolate mixture in a small bowl; beat at medium speed with an electric mixer until smooth. Divide pastry into 6 equal portions. Press each portion onto bottom of an inverted ungreased 8-inch cakepan to within ½ inch of sides. Bake layers, two at a time, at 425° for 5 minutes. Trim uneven edges of circles, if necessary; run a knife under pastry to loosen it from cakepans. Invert layers onto wax paper to cool.

Beat whipping cream until thickened but just before soft peaks form; fold in remaining chocolate mixture. Stack pastry layers on a serving plate, spreading about ⅔ cup whipped cream mixture between each layer. Spoon remaining whipped cream mixture on top of cake; garnish, if desired.

Cover and chill at least 8 hours before serving. Store in refrigerator. Yield: one 8-inch stack cake.

Cookies-and-Cream Cake

½   gallon cookies-and-cream ice cream,
          softened
1   (18.25-ounce) package chocolate cake mix
          without pudding
3   large eggs
1⅓   cups water
½   cup vegetable oil
1   (8-ounce) container frozen whipped topping,
          thawed

Spread ice cream evenly into two 9-inch round cakepans lined with plastic wrap. Place in freezer at least 1 hour. Remove from pans, and return to freezer.

Combine cake mix and next 3 ingredients; beat at low speed with an electric mixer until moistened. Beat at medium speed 2 minutes.

Pour batter into three greased and floured 9-inch round cakepans. Bake at 350° for 20 to 23 minutes or until a wooden pick inserted in center comes out clean. Cool in pans on wire racks 10 minutes; remove from pans, and let cool completely on wire racks.

To assemble cake, remove ice cream from freezer, and remove plastic wrap. Place one cake layer on cake platter; top with ice cream layer. Repeat with second cake layer, ice cream, and third cake layer.

Frost top and sides of cake with whipped topping. Cover and store in freezer. Yield: one 3-layer cake.

Mama Blue's Chocolate Cake

2   cups all-purpose flour
2   cups sugar
¼   cup cocoa
1   teaspoon ground cinnamon
1   cup butter or margarine
1   cup water
1   teaspoon baking soda
2   large eggs, lightly beaten
½   cup buttermilk
1   teaspoon vanilla extract
1   (14-ounce) package miniature chocolate-covered peppermint patties, unwrapped
Bubba's Favorite Frosting

Combine first 4 ingredients; set aside. Combine butter and water in a large saucepan; bring to a boil. Remove from heat; stir in soda. Add flour mixture, stirring well. Stir in eggs, buttermilk, and vanilla. Spoon batter into a greased and floured 13- x 9- x 2-inch pan. Bake at 350° for 30 minutes.

Immediately top cake with candy; bake 2 additional minutes. Gently spread melted candy over cake. Spread Bubba's Favorite Frosting over top. Cut into squares. Yield: 15 servings.

Bubba's Favorite Frosting

½   cup butter or margarine
⅓   cup milk
1   (16-ounce) package powdered sugar, sifted
¼   cup cocoa
1   teaspoon vanilla extract

Combine butter and milk in a large saucepan. Bring to a boil; remove from heat. Combine sugar and cocoa; add to butter mixture. Add vanilla; stir until smooth. Yield: 2 cups.

Smiley Face Chocolate Pound Cake

1   cup butter or margarine, softened
2   cups sugar
1   cup firmly packed brown sugar
6   large eggs
2½   cups all-purpose flour
¼   teaspoon baking soda
½   cup cocoa
1   (8-ounce) carton sour cream
2   teaspoons vanilla extract
Powdered sugar (optional)

Beat butter at medium speed with an electric mixer about 2 minutes. Gradually add sugars, beating 5 to 7 minutes. Add eggs, one at a time, beating just until yellow disappears.

Combine flour, soda, and cocoa; add to creamed mixture alternately with sour cream, beginning and ending with flour mixture. Mix at lowest speed just until blended after each addition. Stir in vanilla. Spoon batter into a greased and floured 10-inch tube pan. Bake at 325° for 1 hour and 20 minutes or until a wooden pick inserted in center comes out clean. Cool in pan on a wire rack 15 minutes; remove from pan, and cool completely on wire rack. Sprinkle with powdered sugar, if desired. Yield: one 10-inch cake.

Thanks, Mama …

for slices of chocolate pound cake in my lunchbox.

Grasshopper Cheesecake

5 (8-ounce) packages cream cheese, softened
1½ cups sugar
3 large eggs
1 (16-ounce) carton sour cream
¼ cup white crème de cacao
¼ cup green crème de menthe
2½ teaspoons vanilla extract
Chocolate Wafer Crust
½ cup whipping cream, whipped
Garnish: chocolaty-mint thin shavings

Thanks, Mama ...

for givin' me my magic shoes— shoes you said could take me anywhere.

Beat cream cheese at high speed with an electric mixer until soft and creamy; gradually add sugar, and beat well.

Add eggs, one at a time, beating after each addition. Stir in sour cream and next 3 ingredients; pour into crust.

Bake at 350° for 40 minutes. Turn oven off, leaving cheesecake in oven 30 minutes. Open oven door; leave in oven 30 minutes. Remove from oven; run a knife around edge. Cool on a wire rack; cover and chill at least 8 hours.

Spread whipped cream around outer edge, and garnish, if desired. Yield: one 10-inch cheesecake.

Chocolate Wafer Crust

1 (9-ounce) box chocolate wafer cookies, crushed (2 cups)
⅓ cup butter or margarine, melted

Combine ingredients; press into a 10-inch springform pan. Bake at 350° for 9 minutes. Yield: one 10-inch crust.

Millionaire Roulage

5   large eggs, separated
1   cup sugar
¼   cup cocoa, divided
1   teaspoon unflavored gelatin
2   tablespoons cold water
1¼   cups whipping cream
2   tablespoons powdered sugar

Grease a 15- x 10- x 1-inch jellyroll pan with vegetable oil; line with wax paper, and grease and flour wax paper.

Beat egg yolks at high speed with an electric mixer until foamy. Gradually add 1 cup sugar, beating until thick. Gradually stir 3 tablespoons cocoa into yolk mixture. Beat egg whites until stiff; fold into chocolate mixture. Spread batter evenly in prepared pan. Bake at 375° for 12 to 15 minutes.

Sift 1 tablespoon cocoa in a 15- x 10-inch rectangle on a towel. When cake is done, loosen from sides of pan, and turn cake out onto towel. Peel off wax paper. Trim edges of cake; discard. Starting at narrow end, roll up cake and towel. Place seam side down on a wire rack; let cool completely.

Sprinkle gelatin over cold water in a saucepan; let stand 1 minute. Cook over low heat; stir until gelatin dissolves.

Beat whipping cream at low speed with an electric mixer, gradually adding dissolved gelatin. Increase mixer speed to medium; beat until mixture begins to thicken. Add powdered sugar, and beat at high speed until soft peaks form.

Unroll cake, and remove towel. Spread whipped cream on cake, leaving a 1-inch margin around edges; reroll cake. Place on a serving plate, seam side down. Yield: 8 servings.

Chocolate-Pecan Torte

4	large eggs, separated
$\frac{1}{2}$	cup sugar
$\frac{2}{3}$	cup all-purpose flour
$\frac{1}{2}$	teaspoon baking soda
$\frac{1}{4}$	teaspoon salt
$\frac{3}{4}$	cup ground pecans
$\frac{1}{3}$	cup cocoa
$\frac{1}{4}$	cup water
1	teaspoon vanilla extract
$\frac{1}{4}$	cup sugar

Chocolate Frosting
$\frac{3}{4}$ cup chopped pecans
Chocolate Glaze
Garnish: chocolate leaves

Grease bottoms only of 2 (9-inch) round cakepans. Line bottoms of pans with wax paper; grease wax paper. Set aside.

Beat egg yolks at high speed with an electric mixer; gradually add ½ cup sugar, beating until mixture is thick and pale. Combine flour and next 4 ingredients; add to yolk mixture alternately with water, beginning and ending with pecan mixture. Stir in vanilla.

Beat egg whites at high speed with an electric mixer until foamy; gradually add ¼ cup sugar, beating until stiff peaks form. Fold into batter. Pour batter into prepared pans. Bake at 375° for 16 to 18 minutes or until a wooden pick inserted in center comes out clean. Cool in pans on wire racks 10 minutes; remove from pans, and let cool completely on wire racks.

Split cake layers in half horizontally to make 4 layers. Place 1 cake layer on serving plate; spread 1 cup Chocolate Frosting on top of layer. Repeat procedure with second and third cake layers and 2 additional cups Chocolate Frosting. Top stack with fourth cake layer. Spread remaining ½ cup Chocolate Frosting on sides of cake; gently press chopped pecans into frosting. Spread Chocolate Glaze over top. Garnish, if desired. Yield: one 9-inch torte.

Chocolate Frosting

⅔   cup sifted powdered sugar
⅓   cup cocoa
2   cups whipping cream
1½   teaspoons vanilla extract

Combine powdered sugar and cocoa in a large mixing bowl; gradually stir in whipping cream. Add vanilla; beat at low speed with an electric mixer until blended. Beat at high speed until stiff peaks form. Yield: 3½ cups.

Chocolate Glaze

2   tablespoons cocoa
2   tablespoons water
1   tablespoon butter or margarine
1   cup sifted powdered sugar
¼   teaspoon vanilla extract

Combine first 3 ingredients in a small saucepan; cook over medium heat, stirring constantly, until mixture thickens. Remove from heat; stir in powdered sugar and vanilla. Yield: ⅓ cup.

Thanks, Mama ...

for helpin' me realize that sometimes we all do things that don't make no sense.

Black-Bottom Cupcakes

Thanks, Mama ...

for bein' there whenever I needed you.

1½	cups all-purpose flour
1	teaspoon baking soda
½	teaspoon salt
1	cup sugar
¼	cup cocoa
1	cup water
⅓	cup vegetable oil
1	tablespoon white vinegar
1	tablespoon vanilla extract
1	(8-ounce) package cream cheese, softened
1	large egg
½	cup sugar
1	(6-ounce) package semisweet chocolate mini-morsels

Combine first 5 ingredients in a large bowl; make a well in center of mixture. Combine water, oil, vinegar, and vanilla; add to dry ingredients, stirring well. Spoon batter into paper-lined miniature muffin pans, filling two-thirds full.

Combine cream cheese and next 2 ingredients, stirring well. Stir in chocolate morsels. Spoon cream cheese mixture evenly over chocolate batter in each muffin cup. Bake at 350° for 10 to 15 minutes. Immediately remove from pans. Yield: 5 dozen.

Chocolate-Pecan Torte, page 34

Crimson Fudge Balls, page 52

"Life is like a box of chocolates"

Candies

At school was also the place I realized that Mama's chocolate candy was better than everybody else's, on account of the other fellers was always tryin' to rob me of it. In fact, that's how I learned to run so fast.

The good thing about candy is you can save it. Pies an' cakes an' stuff is great, too, but they don't last as long as candy, unless you leave the candy out in the sun too long. Also, you can keep your candy in your pocket for a little while, but it's very hard to walk around with a pie or a fudge sundae in your pocket. Know what I mean?

Tex's Chocolate-Nut Teasers

¾   cup pecan pieces, peanut halves,
        slivered almonds, or pistachio pieces,
        toasted
14   ounces Tempered Chocolate (see recipe,
        page 18)
Nut Filling

Spoon about ½ teaspoon nuts into each 1-inch plastic candy mold (molds should be clean and dry). Spoon ¾ teaspoon Tempered Chocolate over nuts in candy mold; spread to cover sides, using an art brush or back of a small spoon. Freeze 10 minutes or until firm.

Carefully spoon about ¾ teaspoon Nut Filling into each chocolate-filled candy mold. Spoon about ½ teaspoon Tempered Chocolate over filling.

Gently tap molds on counter to remove air bubbles. Freeze 10 minutes or until firm. Invert molds, and remove candies. Store candy at cool room temperature. Yield: 4½ dozen.

Nut Filling
1   cup butter or margarine
1   cup sugar
2   tablespoons water
1   tablespoon light corn syrup
⅔   cup finely chopped pecans, peanuts,
        almonds, or pistachios, toasted
½   teaspoon vanilla extract

Melt butter in a heavy saucepan. Gently add sugar, water, and corn syrup, stirring once. Cook over low heat until sugar dissolves, stirring once.

Bring sugar mixture to a boil. Cover, reduce heat to medium, and cook 2 to 3 minutes to wash down sugar crystals from sides of pan. Uncover mixture, and cook to soft ball stage (235°). Remove from heat, and stir in nuts and vanilla. Pour mixture into a greased pan, and let cool completely. Yield: 1¼ cups.

Thanks, Mama ...

for pretendin' not to notice when I didn't do some things as good as other children.

Crème de Menthe Chocolates

1   (14-ounce) can sweetened condensed
       milk
2   tablespoons butter or margarine
¼   cup green crème de menthe
⅛   teaspoon peppermint extract
8   ounces Tempered Chocolate (see recipe,
       page 18)
Green paste food coloring
Royal Icing (see recipe, page 18)

Thanks, Mama ...

for teachin' me to always see the good in things.

Combine condensed milk and butter in a small saucepan; cook over medium heat, stirring constantly, until mixture comes to a boil. Reduce heat, and simmer 5 minutes, stirring constantly, or until mixture is thickened. Remove from heat, and stir in crème de menthe and peppermint extract. Set aside to cool.

Spoon about ½ teaspoon Tempered Chocolate into each 1-inch plastic candy mold (molds should be clean and dry). Spread chocolate to cover bottom and sides of molds, using an art brush or back of a small spoon. Freeze 10 minutes or until firm.

Carefully spoon about ¾ teaspoon crème de menthe filling into each chocolate-filled mold. Spoon about ½ teaspoon Tempered Chocolate over filling.

Gently tap molds on counter to remove air bubbles. Freeze 10 minutes or until firm. Invert molds, and remove candies.

Stir a small amount of food coloring into Royal Icing. Spoon icing into a decorating bag fitted with small round tip No. 2. Drizzle icing over top of each piece of candy.

Store candy in an airtight container at cool room temperature. Yield: 3 dozen.

Variation: Raspberry Cream Chocolates

Prepare recipe for Crème de Menthe Chocolates, omitting peppermint extract, substituting crème de framboise for crème de menthe, and substituting red food coloring for green in Royal Icing. Add red food coloring to filling mixture, if desired.

White Chocolate Surprises

⅓   cup whipping cream
1½   tablespoons sour cream
8   ounces grated white chocolate or vanilla-flavored
       baking bars
About ½ cup sifted powdered sugar
12   ounces Tempered Chocolate (see recipe, page 18)
2   ounces grated white chocolate or vanilla-flavored
       baking bars, melted

Bring whipping cream to a simmer in a heavy saucepan.
Reduce heat to low, and stir in sour cream. Add 8 ounces
grated white chocolate; stir until chocolate melts, and remove
mixture from heat. Pour mixture into a buttered 8-inch
square pan, and freeze 20 minutes or until firm enough to
hold its shape.
    Place a large piece of wax paper on a baking sheet, and
sprinkle with small amount powdered sugar. Spoon white
chocolate mixture into mounds (about ¾ teaspoon) on wax
paper, and freeze 10 minutes or until almost firm.
    Roll each mound of candy in powdered sugar to make a
ball; set aside.
    Spoon about ½ teaspoon Tempered Chocolate into each
1-inch plastic candy mold (molds should be clean and dry).
Spread chocolate to cover bottom and sides of molds, using
an art brush or back of a small spoon. Freeze 10 minutes or
until firm.
    Carefully place 1 ball of white chocolate filling into each
chocolate-filled candy mold, pressing gently to flatten. Spoon
about ½ teaspoon Tempered Chocolate over filling.
    Gently tap molds on counter to remove air bubbles.
Freeze 10 minutes or until firm. Invert molds, and remove
candies.

Spoon 2 ounces melted white chocolate into a decorating bag fitted with small round tip No. 2. Drizzle white chocolate over top of each piece of candy. Store at cool room temperature. Yield: 3½ dozen.

Note: Mama used white chocolate sold in bulk at candy counters of large department stores or vanilla-flavored baking bars sold in grocery stores for this recipe.

Thanks, Mama ...

*for makin' me eat
all of my peas
and carrots.*

Real Good Chocolate Caramels

2   cups sugar
1½   cups half-and-half
½   cup light corn syrup
¼   cup butter or margarine
1   teaspoon vanilla extract
14   ounces Tempered Chocolate (see recipe, page 18)
Brown paste food coloring
Royal Icing (see recipe, page 18)

Thanks, Mama ...

for standin' up for me 'til I was big enough to do it myself.

Combine first 4 ingredients in a large heavy saucepan; cook over low heat, stirring gently, until sugar dissolves. Cover and cook over medium heat 2 to 3 minutes to wash down sugar crystals from sides of pan. Uncover and cook to firm ball stage (246°). Stir in vanilla; remove from heat. Pour into a buttered 8-inch square pan, without stirring; let cool. Remove from pan; shape mixture into ¾-inch balls.

Spoon about ½ teaspoon Tempered Chocolate into each 1-inch plastic candy mold (molds should be clean and dry). Spread chocolate to cover bottom and sides of molds, using an art brush or back of a small spoon. Freeze 10 minutes or until firm.

Carefully place 1 caramel ball into each chocolate-filled candy mold, pressing caramel gently to flatten. Spoon about ½ teaspoon Tempered Chocolate over filling.

Gently tap molds on counter to remove air bubbles. Freeze 10 minutes or until firm. Invert molds, and remove candies.

Stir a small amount of food coloring into Royal Icing to color icing like caramel. Spoon icing into a decorating bag fitted with small round tip No. 2. Drizzle icing over top of each piece of candy. Store at cool room temperature. Let stand 24 hours before serving for caramel to soften. Yield: 5½ dozen.

Peanut Butter-Chocolate Balls

1½   cups graham cracker crumbs
1½   cups flaked coconut
1½   cups chopped peanuts or pecans
1   cup butter or margarine, melted
1   (16-ounce) package powdered sugar, sifted
1   (12-ounce) jar chunky peanut butter
1   teaspoon vanilla extract
2   (12-ounce) packages semisweet chocolate morsels
3   tablespoons shortening

Combine first 7 ingredients, stirring well. Shape mixture into 1-inch balls.

Combine chocolate morsels and shortening in top of double boiler; bring water to a boil. Reduce heat to low; cook until chocolate melts. Dip each peanut butter ball into chocolate mixture. Place on wax paper to cool. Store in refrigerator. Yield: about 9 dozen.

Note: Mama always froze extra Peanut Butter-Chocolate Balls in an airtight container for later use. She removed them from the freezer about one hour before she told me about them so they could thaw.

Forrest's Four-Chips Fudge

¾   cup butter or margarine
1   (14-ounce) can sweetened condensed milk
3   tablespoons milk
1   (12-ounce) package semisweet chocolate
     morsels
1   (11½-ounce) package milk chocolate morsels
1   (10-ounce) package peanut butter-flavored
     morsels
1   cup butterscotch-flavored morsels
1   (7-ounce) jar marshmallow cream
1½   teaspoons vanilla extract
½ to 1 teaspoon almond extract
1   pound walnuts, coarsely chopped

Melt butter in a heavy Dutch oven over low heat; stir in condensed milk and milk. Add all morsels, stirring constantly, until mixture is smooth. Remove from heat; stir in marshmallow cream and flavorings. Stir in walnuts.

    Spoon mixture into a buttered 15- x 10- x 1-inch jellyroll pan; spread evenly. Cover and chill; cut into squares. Store in refrigerator. Yield: 5 pounds.

Chocolate Fudge-in-a-Flash

3   cups semisweet chocolate morsels
1   (14-ounce) can sweetened condensed
        milk
¼   cup butter or margarine, cut into pieces
1   cup chopped walnuts

Combine first 3 ingredients in a 2-quart glass bowl. Microwave at MEDIUM (50% power) 4 to 5 minutes, stirring at 1½-minute intervals. Stir in walnuts.

    Pour mixture into a buttered 8-inch square dish. Cover and chill at least 2 hours; cut into squares. Yield: 2 pounds.

Thanks, Mama ...

*for lettin' me
spend so much
time with Jenny.*

Orange-Walnut Fudge

3	cups sugar
½	cup orange juice
½	cup water
1	(12-ounce) package semisweet chocolate morsels
1	tablespoon grated orange rind
4	cups coarsely chopped walnuts

Thanks, Mama ...

for always givin' me extra marshmallows in my hot chocolate.

Combine first 3 ingredients in a large saucepan. Cook over medium heat, stirring constantly, until sugar dissolves and mixture boils. Cook to softball stage (234°), stirring occasionally. Remove from heat. Add chocolate morsels and orange rind; stir until chocolate melts. Stir in walnuts. Pour into a buttered 13- x 9- x 2-inch pan; cool. Cut into 1-inch squares, and store in an airtight container at room temperature. Yield: 9 dozen.

Southern Peanut Butter Fudge

¼   cup butter or margarine
⅓   cup milk
1   teaspoon vanilla extract
1   (16-ounce) package powdered sugar
½   cup cocoa
¼   teaspoon salt
½   cup chunky peanut butter

Melt butter in a medium saucepan; remove from heat, and add milk and vanilla.

Sift powdered sugar, cocoa, and salt together; gradually add powdered sugar mixture to milk mixture, stirring until blended. Stir in peanut butter. Press mixture into a buttered 8-inch square pan. Cover and chill; cut into squares. Yield: about 2 dozen.

Crimson Fudge Balls

1   (8-ounce) package cream cheese, softened
1   (6-ounce) package semisweet chocolate morsels, melted
¾   cup vanilla wafer crumbs
¼   cup strawberry preserves
½   cup almonds, toasted and finely chopped

Beat cream cheese at medium speed with an electric mixer until creamy. Add melted chocolate, beating until smooth. Stir in vanilla wafer crumbs and strawberry preserves; cover and chill 1 hour. Shape into 1-inch balls; roll in chopped almonds. Store in an airtight container in the refrigerator up to 1 week or freeze up to 2 months. Yield: 4 dozen.

'Bama Bittersweet Truffles

½   cup butter or margarine
¾   cup cocoa
1   (14-ounce) can sweetened condensed milk
1   teaspoon vanilla extract
Cocoa

Melt butter in a heavy saucepan over low heat; stir in ¾ cup cocoa. Gradually add condensed milk, stirring constantly, until smooth. Cook over medium heat, stirring constantly, until thickened and smooth (about 3 minutes). Remove from heat; stir in vanilla. Pour mixture into a lightly greased 8-inch square pan. Cover and chill 3 hours or until firm.

    Shape mixture into 1¼-inch balls; roll in additional cocoa. Place balls in miniature paper baking cups. Store in an airtight container in the refrigerator up to 1 week. Yield: 3 dozen.

Thanks, Mama ...

*for teachin' me to
always do what
I gotta do.*

Chocolate-Mint Truffles

1	(12-ounce) package semisweet chocolate morsels
1/4	cup egg substitute
1/4	cup plus 2 tablespoons butter or margarine, cut into cubes
1/4	cup plus 2 tablespoons sifted powdered sugar
1/2	teaspoon mint extract
16	ounces chocolate-flavored candy coating
4	ounces vanilla-flavored candy coating, melted

Thanks, Mama ...

for always believin' in me.

Place chocolate morsels in top of a double boiler; bring water to a boil. Reduce heat to low; cook until chocolate melts. Remove top of double boiler from hot water.

Beat egg substitute 1 minute. Gradually stir about one-fourth of hot chocolate into egg substitute; add to remaining hot mixture, stirring constantly. Add butter, sugar, and mint extract; beat at medium speed with an electric mixer until butter melts and mixture is smooth. Cover and chill 1 hour.

Shape mixture into 1-inch balls; cover and chill 1 hour or until firm.

Place chocolate candy coating in top of double boiler; bring water to a boil. Reduce heat to low; cook until coating melts. Remove from heat, leaving top of double boiler over hot water. Dip each ball of candy into coating, letting excess coating drip off. Place on wax paper-lined baking sheets, and chill until coating hardens. Drizzle truffles with melted vanilla candy coating. Yield: about 3 dozen.

Chocolate-Mint Truffles, page 54

Candy Bar Brownies, page 58

Cookies

There's 'bout a hundrid kinds of cookies an' I bet Mama made every one of 'em, one time or the other. Chocolate chip was my favorite. One reason I done pretty good in school is because when I went up to do my homework at night, I could smell cookies in the oven, an' when I was finished, Mama'd let me come down an' fix me a glass of milk an' I'd eat the chocolate chip cookies straight from the oven—with the chocolate still warm an' gooey, ya know? I always got through with my homework on them nights. Thanks, Mama.

Candy Bar Brownies

4	large eggs, lightly beaten
2	cups sugar
¾	cup butter or margarine, melted
2	teaspoons vanilla extract
1½	cups all-purpose flour
½	teaspoon baking powder
¼	teaspoon salt
⅓	cup cocoa
4	(2.07-ounce) chocolate-coated caramel-peanut nougat bars, coarsely chopped
3	(1.55-ounce) milk chocolate bars, finely chopped

Combine first 4 ingredients in a large bowl. Combine flour and next 3 ingredients; stir into sugar mixture. Fold in chopped nougat bars.

Spoon batter into a greased and floured 13- x 9- x 2-inch pan; sprinkle with chopped milk chocolate bars. Bake at 350° for 30 to 35 minutes. Cool on a wire rack, and cut into squares. Yield: 2½ dozen.

Note: For chocolate-coated caramel-peanut nougat bars, Mama always used Snickers, and for milk chocolate bars, she used Hershey's.

Feather-Light Fudge Brownies

1½   cups sugar
½   cup egg substitute
¼   cup margarine, melted
2   tablespoons water
1   teaspoon vanilla extract
1¼   cups sifted cake flour
½   cup cocoa
1   teaspoon baking powder
Dash of salt
¾   cup semisweet chocolate morsels
Vegetable cooking spray

Combine first 5 ingredients in a large bowl, stirring well.
Combine flour, cocoa, baking powder, and salt; add to sugar
mixture, stirring well. Stir in chocolate morsels.

    Spoon batter into a 9-inch square pan coated with cook-
ing spray. Bake at 325° for 30 minutes. Cool on a wire rack,
and cut into squares. Yield: 16 brownies.

Thanks, Mama …

*for makin' me
realize that
sometimes there
are things that
we just can't
change.*

Forrest's Favorite Fudge Brownies

2½   cups sugar
1½   cups butter or margarine
5   (1-ounce) squares unsweetened chocolate
6   large eggs, lightly beaten
2   cups all-purpose flour
1   cup coarsely chopped macadamia nuts or almonds
Fudge Frosting
Garnish: chopped macadamia nuts

Thanks, Mama ...

for teachin' me to treat everybody the same.

Combine first 3 ingredients in a large saucepan; cook over low heat until chocolate melts, stirring often. Remove from heat, and cool 10 minutes. Stir in eggs, flour, and nuts.

Pour batter into a greased and floured 13- x 9- x 2-inch pan. Bake at 350° for 30 to 35 minutes. Cool on a wire rack.

Pour Fudge Frosting over top; chill 15 minutes, and cut into squares. Garnish, if desired. Yield: 4 dozen.

Fudge Frosting

1   cup whipping cream
12   (1-ounce) squares semisweet chocolate

Heat whipping cream in a medium saucepan over medium heat; add chocolate, stirring until smooth. Remove from heat, and cool to room temperature. Yield: 2½ cups.

Southern Mint Julep Brownies

4	(1-ounce) squares unsweetened chocolate
1	cup butter or margarine
4	large eggs
2	cups sugar
1½	cups all-purpose flour
½	teaspoon salt
2	tablespoons bourbon
1	teaspoon peppermint extract
1	tablespoon powdered sugar

Garnish: fresh mint leaves

Combine chocolate and butter in a heavy saucepan; cook over low heat, stirring constantly, until chocolate melts. Let stand 10 minutes.

Beat eggs at medium speed with an electric mixer until thick and pale (about 2 minutes); gradually add sugar, beating well. Add chocolate mixture, flour, and next 3 ingredients; beat at low speed 1 minute.

Spoon batter into a lightly greased and floured 13- x 9- x 2-inch pan. Bake at 350° for 25 to 30 minutes or until a wooden pick inserted in center comes out clean. Cool on a wire rack 10 minutes. Sprinkle brownies with powdered sugar; cut into bars. Garnish, if desired. Yield: 4 dozen.

Triple-Decker Brownies

1½   cups quick-cooking oats, toasted
1   cup all-purpose flour
1   cup firmly packed brown sugar
½   teaspoon baking soda
¼   teaspoon salt
¾   cup butter or margarine, melted
2   (1-ounce) squares unsweetened chocolate
½   cup butter or margarine
1½   cups sugar
2   large eggs
1⅓   cups all-purpose flour
½   teaspoon baking powder
¼   teaspoon salt
½   cup milk
1   teaspoon vanilla extract
1   cup chopped pecans
Chocolate Frosting

Combine first 5 ingredients in a large bowl; add ¾ cup melted butter, stirring well. Press mixture into bottom of two greased 8-inch square pans. Bake at 350° for 10 minutes.

    Melt chocolate and ½ cup butter in a large heavy saucepan over low heat; remove from heat. Add sugar and eggs, mixing well. Combine 1⅓ cups flour, baking powder, and ¼ teaspoon salt; add to chocolate mixture alternately with milk. Stir in vanilla and pecans.

    Spread batter over crust, and bake at 350° for 20 to 25 minutes. Cool on wire racks. Spread with Chocolate Frosting. Cut into 2-inch squares. Yield: 32 brownies.

Chocolate Frosting

2   (1-ounce) squares unsweetened chocolate
¼   cup butter or margarine
3   cups sifted powdered sugar
2   teaspoons vanilla extract
¼   cup hot water, divided

Melt chocolate and butter in a heavy saucepan over low heat; remove from heat. Stir in powdered sugar, vanilla, and 1 tablespoon water. Stir in an additional 2 to 3 tablespoons water until frosting is desired spreading consistency. Yield: 1½ cups.

Thanks, Mama …

*for always
makin' time
for me.*

Butter Pecan Turtle Bars

½   cup butter or margarine, softened
1   cup firmly packed brown sugar
2   cups all-purpose flour
1   cup chopped pecans
⅔   cup butter or margarine, melted
½   cup firmly packed brown sugar
1   cup milk chocolate morsels

Thanks, Mama ...

*for always lettin'
me lick the
beaters when
you made
cookies and
cakes—'specially
if they was
chocolate.*

Beat ½ cup butter at medium speed with an electric mixer
until creamy; add 1 cup brown sugar, beating well. Gradually
add flour, mixing well. Press mixture into an ungreased
13- x 9- x 2-inch pan. Sprinkle with pecans. Set aside.

Combine ⅔ cup butter and ½ cup brown sugar in a
small saucepan. Bring to a boil over medium heat, stirring
constantly. Boil 30 seconds, stirring constantly. Remove from
heat, and pour mixture over crust.

Bake at 350° for 18 minutes or until bubbly. Remove
from oven; immediately sprinkle with chocolate morsels. Let
stand 2 to 3 minutes; swirl chocolate gently with a knife to
create a marbled effect. Cool on a wire rack, and cut into bars.
Yield: 4 dozen.

Rt. 17 Chocolate Chip Squares

2   (20-ounce) rolls refrigerated chocolate chip cookie
        dough
2   (8-ounce) packages cream cheese, softened
1½ cups sugar
2   large eggs

Freeze rolls of cookie dough; slice 1 roll of frozen cookie dough into 40 (⅛-inch) slices. Arrange cookie slices in a well-greased 15- x 10- x 1-inch jellyroll pan. Press cookie dough together to form bottom crust. Set aside.

Beat cream cheese at high speed with an electric mixer until light and fluffy; gradually add sugar, and mix well. Add eggs, one at a time, beating after each addition. Pour mixture onto cookie layer.

Slice remaining dough into 40 (⅛-inch) slices; arrange over cream cheese mixture. Bake at 350° for 45 minutes. Cool on a wire rack, and cut into squares. Yield: 4 dozen.

German Chocolate Chess Squares

1   (18.25-ounce) package German chocolate cake
       mix with pudding
1   large egg, lightly beaten
½   cup butter or margarine, melted
1   cup chopped pecans
1   (8-ounce) package cream cheese, softened
2   large eggs
1   (16-ounce) package powdered sugar,
       sifted

Combine first 4 ingredients in a large bowl, stirring until dry ingredients are moistened. Press into bottom of a greased 13- x 9- x 2-inch pan; set aside.

Combine cream cheese, 2 eggs, and 1 cup powdered sugar; beat at medium speed with an electric mixer until blended. Gradually add remaining powdered sugar, beating after each addition. Pour over chocolate layer, spreading evenly.

Bake at 350° for 40 minutes. Cool on a wire rack, and cut into squares. Yield: 4 dozen.

Yummy Bars

1   (14-ounce) package caramels, unwrapped
1   (5-ounce) can evaporated milk, divided
1   (18.25-ounce) package German chocolate
      cake mix with pudding
¾   cup butter or margarine, melted
1   large egg
1   (6-ounce) package semisweet chocolate morsels
1   cup coarsely chopped pecans

Combine caramels and ¼ cup evaporated milk in a small saucepan. Cook over low heat until smooth, stirring occasionally; set aside.

Combine cake mix, butter, egg, and remaining evaporated milk. Spoon half of mixture into a greased 13- x 9- x 2-inch pan, spreading mixture evenly; bake at 350° for 6 minutes. Remove from oven; sprinkle with morsels and pecans. Spoon caramel mixture on top; carefully spoon remaining cake mixture over caramel layer.

Bake at 350° for 20 to 25 minutes. Cool cake on a wire rack, and cut into bars. Yield: about 3 dozen.

Thanks, Mama ...

for teachin' me that people might do bad things, like callin' me names, but that don't mean they're bad. Maybe they just don't know better.

Kissy Cookies

1   large egg, lightly beaten
1   cup chunky peanut butter
1   cup sugar
36   milk chocolate kisses, unwrapped

Combine first 3 ingredients; shape into ¾-inch balls. Place on ungreased baking sheets; bake at 350° for 10 minutes. Immediately press a chocolate kiss in center of each cookie; remove to wire racks to cool. Yield: 3 dozen.

Thanks, Mama ...

for teachin' me that you never know what you're gonna get. So make the best of what you got.

Jenny's Choco-Chewies

1   teaspoon instant coffee granules
1   teaspoon hot water
3   egg whites, slightly beaten
½   teaspoon vanilla extract
3   cups sifted powdered sugar
⅔   cup cocoa
2   tablespoons all-purpose flour
⅛   teaspoon salt
2   cups finely chopped pecans

Dissolve coffee granules in hot water in a bowl; stir in egg whites and vanilla. Combine sugar and next 3 ingredients. Add egg white mixture; beat at medium speed with an electric mixer until blended. Stir in pecans.

Drop dough by rounded teaspoonfuls 1 inch apart onto greased and floured baking sheets. Bake at 350° for 12 to 15 minutes. Remove to wire racks to cool. Yield: 4 dozen.

Mobile Mint Cookies

⅔   cup butter or margarine, softened
1   cup sugar
⅓   cup firmly packed dark brown sugar
1   large egg
1   teaspoon vanilla extract
1   (1-ounce) square unsweetened chocolate, melted
1½   cups all-purpose flour
1   (10-ounce) package mint chocolate morsels

Beat butter at medium speed with an electric mixer until
fluffy; gradually add sugars, beating well. Add egg, vanilla,
and melted chocolate, mixing well. Gradually add flour,
mixing well. Stir in morsels.

Drop dough by level tablespoonfuls onto lightly greased
baking sheets. Bake at 325° for 12 to 15 minutes. Cool
on baking sheets 3 minutes; remove to wire racks to cool
completely. Yield: 3½ dozen.

Peanut-Oat Chocolate Chippers

½   cup butter or margarine, softened
1   (18-ounce) jar chunky peanut butter
1½   cups sugar
1½   cups firmly packed brown sugar
4   large eggs
1   teaspoon vanilla extract
6   cups quick-cooking oats, uncooked
2½   teaspoons baking soda
1   (6-ounce) package semisweet chocolate morsels

Beat butter and peanut butter at medium speed with an electric mixer until fluffy; gradually add sugars, beating well. Add eggs and vanilla, mixing well. Combine oats and baking soda; add to butter mixture, mixing well. Stir in chocolate morsels.

Drop dough by tablespoonfuls onto ungreased baking sheets. Bake at 350° for 9 to 10 minutes. Cool on baking sheets 5 minutes; remove to wire racks to cool completely. Yield: 7 dozen.

Chocolate Surprise Cookies

1   cup butter or margarine, softened
1   cup sugar
1   cup firmly packed brown sugar
2   large eggs
2¼   cups all-purpose flour
¾   cup cocoa
1   teaspoon baking soda
2   teaspoons vanilla extract
1   cup chopped pecans, divided
1   tablespoon sugar
1   (9-ounce) package chewy caramels in milk chocolate

Beat butter at medium speed with an electric mixer until creamy. Gradually add sugars, beating well. Add eggs, beating well.

Combine flour, cocoa, and soda; add to butter mixture, mixing well. Stir in vanilla and ½ cup chopped pecans. Cover cookie dough, and refrigerate 1 hour.

Combine remaining ½ cup pecans and 1 tablespoon sugar; set aside. Gently press 1 tablespoon cookie dough around each candy, forming a ball. Dip 1 side of cookie in pecan mixture. Place, pecan side up, 2 inches apart on ungreased baking sheets. Bake at 375° for 8 minutes. (Cookies will look soft.) Let cool 1 minute on baking sheets; remove to wire racks to cool completely. Yield: 4 dozen.

Thanks, Mama ...

for leavin' the nuts out of the chocolate chip cookies when I was little, 'cause I liked 'em better that way, even if you didn't.

Chunky Hazelnut-Toffee Cookies

1 cup unsalted butter, softened
¾ cup firmly packed brown sugar
½ cup sugar
2 large eggs
1 tablespoon vanilla extract
2¾ cups all-purpose flour
1½ teaspoons baking powder
½ teaspoon baking soda
½ teaspoon salt
4 (1.4 ounce) English toffee-flavored candy bars, chopped
2 (10-ounce) packages semisweet chocolate chunks
1 cup toasted, chopped hazelnuts or pecans

Thanks, Mama ...

for the plate of cookies that was always there when I came home from school.

Beat butter at medium speed with an electric mixer until creamy. Gradually add sugars, beating well. Add eggs and vanilla, beating well.

 Combine flour and next 3 ingredients, stirring well. Add to butter mixture, beating at low speed just until blended. Stir in toffee candy, chocolate chunks, and nuts.

 Drop dough by heaping tablespoonfuls 1½ inches apart onto ungreased baking sheets. Bake at 350° for 10 minutes or until lightly browned. Let cool slightly on baking sheets; remove to wire racks to cool completely. Yield: 4½ dozen.

Note: For English toffee-flavored candy bars, Mama always used Heath bars.

Chunky Hazelnut-Toffee Cookies, page 72

Chocolate Decadence, page 76

"Life is like a box of chocolates"

Creamy Creations

*Just to show you how good it was, one time
I broke a date with my Jenny just so's I could wait
around for Mama's "Feathery" Chocolate Soufflé to
come out of the oven! An' durin' the summers,
she'd make chocolate ice cream, too, out on the
back porch, an' sometimes I'd get to turn the
crank—which I never did mind 'cause I knew when
we was done I'd get to lick the paddle.*

   *Mama could make chocolate whipped cream,
too, but one time I got in trouble 'cause she was
savin' a big bowl of it in the icebox for her bridge
club an' I found it an' ate it all up. But she didn't
spank me, an' I'll always remember her for that.*

Chocolate Decadence

16   (1-ounce) squares semisweet chocolate
⅔   cup butter
5   large eggs
2   tablespoons sugar
2   tablespoons all-purpose flour
2   cups fresh raspberries
2   cups water
¼   cup sugar
2   tablespoons cornstarch
2   tablespoons water
Whipped cream
Garnish: fresh raspberries

Line the bottom of a 9-inch springform pan with parchment paper; set aside.

Combine chocolate and butter in top of a double boiler; bring water to a boil. Reduce heat to low; cook until chocolate melts.

Place eggs in a large mixing bowl. Gradually add chocolate mixture to eggs, beating at medium speed with an electric mixer 10 minutes. Fold in 2 tablespoons sugar and flour.

Pour batter into prepared pan. Bake at 400° for 15 minutes. (Dessert will not be set in center.) Remove from oven; cover and chill thoroughly.

Combine 2 cups raspberries, 2 cups water, and ¼ cup sugar in a large saucepan; bring mixture to a boil over medium-high heat. Reduce heat, and simmer 30 minutes, stirring occasionally. Pour raspberry mixture through a wire-mesh strainer into a bowl; discard seeds. Return raspberry mixture to pan.

Combine cornstarch and 2 tablespoons water; add to raspberry mixture. Cook over medium heat, stirring constantly, until mixture comes to a boil; boil 1 minute, stirring constantly. Cool completely.

To serve, spoon 2 to 3 tablespoons raspberry sauce on each individual dessert plate; place wedge of chocolate dessert on sauce. Top each wedge with a dollop of whipped cream. Garnish, if desired. Yield: 10 to 12 servings.

Thanks, Mama ...

for goin' to a lot of trouble so's I could get an education.

Feathery Chocolate Soufflé

Butter
2   tablespoons butter
1   (1-ounce) square unsweetened chocolate
2   tablespoons all-purpose flour
½   cup milk
Dash of salt
2   large eggs, separated
¼   cup sugar
½   teaspoon vanilla extract
Mocha Cream

Thanks, Mama ...

for not bein' mad when I drank all the Dr Pepper.

Coat bottom and sides of a 2-cup soufflé dish or 2 (10-ounce) custard cups with butter. Set aside.

Melt 2 tablespoons butter and chocolate in a saucepan over medium heat; add flour, stirring until smooth. Cook 1 minute, stirring constantly. Gradually add milk; cook, stirring constantly, until thickened and bubbly. Stir in salt; remove from heat. Beat yolks and sugar at medium speed with an electric mixer until thick and pale. Stir in vanilla. Gradually stir about one-fourth of hot chocolate mixture into yolk mixture; beat at medium speed until blended. Gradually add remaining hot chocolate mixture, mixing constantly.

Beat egg whites until soft peaks form. Gently fold about one-fourth of egg whites into chocolate mixture; fold remaining egg whites into chocolate mixture. Carefully spoon into prepared soufflé dish or custard cups. Bake at 325° for 35 minutes or until puffed and set. Serve immediately with Mocha Cream. Yield: 2 servings.

Mocha Cream

½   cup whipping cream
1   tablespoon sugar
1½   teaspoons cocoa
½   teaspoon instant coffee granules

Combine all ingredients in a small mixing bowl; beat at high speed with an electric mixer until soft peaks form; cover and chill. Yield: 1 cup.

Fudge Dessert with Kahlúa Cream

2   cups sugar
½   cup all-purpose flour
¾   cup cocoa
1   cup butter or margarine, melted
5   large eggs, slightly beaten
2   teaspoons vanilla extract
1½   cups chopped pecans
Kahlúa Cream

Combine first 6 ingredients in a large mixing bowl; beat 3 to 4 minutes at medium speed with an electric mixer. Stir in pecans. Spoon into 10 lightly greased 6-ounce soufflé dishes or custard cups. Place dishes in a shallow pan; pour warm water to depth of 1 inch into pan. Bake at 300° for 40 minutes or until tops are crusty. Remove dishes from water, and cool. Dollop or pipe Kahlúa Cream on top. Yield: 10 servings.

Kahlúa Cream

1   cup whipping cream
3   tablespoons Kahlúa or other coffee-flavored liqueur
½   cup sifted powdered sugar

Combine all ingredients in a small mixing bowl; beat at medium speed with an electric mixer until soft peaks form. Yield: 2¼ cups.

Bubba's Chocolate Cake Pudding

1   cup all-purpose flour
2   teaspoons baking powder
⅛   teaspoon salt
¾   cup sugar
2   tablespoons cocoa
½   cup milk
3   tablespoons butter or margarine, melted
1   teaspoon vanilla extract
½   cup sugar
½   cup firmly packed brown sugar
¼   cup cocoa
1½   cups water
Sweetened whipped cream or ice cream (optional)

Combine first 5 ingredients in a greased 9-inch square pan, stirring well. Stir in milk, butter, and vanilla, spreading mixture evenly in pan.

Combine ½ cup sugar, ½ cup brown sugar, and ¼ cup cocoa, and sprinkle mixture evenly over batter. Pour water over top. Bake pudding at 350° for 40 minutes. Serve with sweetened whipped cream or ice cream, if desired. Yield: 6 servings.

Thanks, Mama ...

for comin' to all my college football games. Who would have believed that after only five years I got a college degree?

Pots de Crème

2   cups half-and-half
2   large eggs, lightly beaten
2   tablespoons sugar
3⅓   cups semisweet chocolate morsels
3   tablespoons amaretto or other almond-flavored liqueur
2   teaspoons vanilla extract
Pinch of salt
Garnishes: whipped cream, chocolate shavings

Combine first 3 ingredients in a heavy saucepan; cook over medium heat 12 minutes or until temperature reaches 160°. Add chocolate morsels and next 3 ingredients, stirring until smooth. Spoon into individual serving containers; cover and chill. Garnish, if desired. Yield: 5 to 6 servings.

Thanks, Mama ...

for listenin' when I talked about missin' my beautiful Jenny.

Paddle Wheelin' Parfait

1	cup milk chocolate morsels
¼	cup whipping cream
2	tablespoons water
2	teaspoons vanilla extract
1½	cups whipping cream, whipped
1	cup vanilla wafers, crushed

Combine first 3 ingredients in a heavy saucepan; cook over low heat, stirring constantly, until chocolate melts. Cool. Stir in vanilla, and fold in whipped cream.

Layer mousse and vanilla wafer crumbs into 6 (4-ounce) parfait glasses. Cover and freeze at least 1 hour or up to 2 days. Let stand 10 to 15 minutes before serving. Yield: 6 servings.

All-American Chocolate Ice Cream

3   large eggs
1   cup sugar
4   cups half-and-half
2   cups whipping cream
1   cup chocolate syrup
1   tablespoon vanilla extract
About 3 cups milk

Beat eggs at medium speed with an electric mixer until frothy. Gradually add sugar, beating until thick. Add half-and-half and next 3 ingredients; mix well. Pour mixture into a large heavy saucepan. Cook over medium heat until mixture comes to a boil; boil 1 minute. Let mixture cool.

Pour mixture into freezer can of a 1-gallon hand-turned or electric freezer. Add enough milk to fill can about three-fourths full. Freeze according to manufacturer's instructions. Pack freezer with ice and rock salt, and let stand 1 hour. Yield: about 1 gallon.

Medal of Honor Hot Fudge Sundae

¼   cup butter or margarine
1½   cups semisweet chocolate morsels, divided
¾   cup sugar
⅔   cup all-purpose flour
¼   teaspoon baking powder
¼   teaspoon salt
2   large eggs, lightly beaten
½   teaspoon vanilla extract
½   cup chopped pecans
Ice cream
Easy Hot Fudge Sauce

Combine butter and 1 cup chocolate morsels in a heavy
saucepan. Cook over low heat, stirring constantly, until
chocolate and butter melt. Remove from heat. Add sugar and
next 5 ingredients, stirring until blended. Stir in pecans and
remaining ½ cup chocolate morsels.
    Spread mixture into a lightly greased 8-inch square
pan. Bake at 350° for 30 minutes or until center is set. Cool
in pan on a wire rack. Cut into squares; serve with ice cream
and warm Easy Hot Fudge Sauce. Yield: 16 servings.

Easy Hot Fudge Sauce

1   (12-ounce) package semisweet chocolate morsels
1   (12-ounce) can evaporated milk
1   cup sugar
1   tablespoon butter or margarine
1   teaspoon vanilla extract

Combine first 3 ingredients in a heavy saucepan. Stir constantly over medium heat until chocolate melts and mixture
comes to a boil. Stir in butter and vanilla. Yield: 3 cups.

Thanks, Mama ...

*for tellin' me that
there's only so
much a person
really needs, an'
the rest is just for
showin' off.*

Delta Ice Cream Dessert

1¼   cups cream-filled chocolate sandwich cookie
         crumbs
3   tablespoons butter or margarine, melted
Caramel Sauce
1   quart chocolate ice cream, softened
1   quart vanilla ice cream, softened
6   (1.4-ounce) English toffee-flavored candy bars,
         crushed
Chocolate Sauce
1   quart coffee ice cream, softened

Thanks, Mama ...

*for that fudge
you sent to me at
boot camp —
Bubba an' me
liked that
real good.*

Combine cookie crumbs and butter, mixing well. Press crumb
mixture firmly over bottom of a 10-inch springform pan. Bake
at 350° for 6 minutes. Cool on a wire rack.

Spread ½ cup Caramel Sauce over crust, leaving a
1-inch border; freeze until set. Spread chocolate ice cream
over Caramel Sauce; freeze until firm.

Combine vanilla ice cream and crushed candy bars.
Spread mixture over chocolate ice cream; freeze until firm.
Spread 1 cup Chocolate Sauce over vanilla ice cream; freeze
until set.

Spread coffee ice cream over Chocolate Sauce. Cover
tightly, and freeze at least 8 hours.

Remove dessert from freezer 10 minutes before serving;
remove sides of springform pan, and slice dessert into
wedges. Serve with the remaining sauces. Yield: 12 to 14
servings.

Caramel Sauce

⅓   cup butter or margarine
2   cups firmly packed brown sugar
⅛   teaspoon salt
1   cup half-and-half, divided
2   teaspoons cornstarch
2   teaspoons vanilla extract

Combine butter, brown sugar, salt, and ¾ cup half-and-half in a heavy saucepan. Cook over low heat, stirring constantly, until sugar dissolves. Do not boil. Combine cornstarch and remaining ¼ cup half-and-half; gradually stir into brown sugar mixture. Cook over low heat, stirring constantly, until mixture thickens. Stir in vanilla. Yield: 2 cups.

Chocolate Sauce

1   (6-ounce) package semisweet chocolate
       morsels
1   (12-ounce) can evaporated milk
2   cups sifted powdered sugar

Combine chocolate morsels and evaporated milk in a small heavy saucepan. Cook over medium heat, stirring constantly, until chocolate morsels melt. Stir in powdered sugar. Cook mixture over medium heat 5 minutes or until sauce thickens, stirring frequently. Yield: 2 cups.

Note: For English toffee-flavored candy bars, Mama always used Heath bars.

Ice Cream Angel Dessert

1   (10-inch) angel food cake
4   cups chocolate-mint ice cream, softened and divided
2   cups pink peppermint ice cream, softened
Whipped Cream Frosting
Chocolate-Mint Sauce

Split cake horizontally into 4 equal layers. Place bottom cake layer on a serving plate; spread top of layer with half of chocolate-mint ice cream to within ½ inch from edge. Top with second cake layer; cover and freeze 45 minutes or until firm. Spread second cake layer with pink peppermint ice cream. Add third cake layer; cover and freeze 45 minutes or until firm. Spread third layer with remaining chocolate-mint ice cream, and top with remaining cake layer; freeze 45 minutes or until firm.

Spread Whipped Cream Frosting on top and sides of cake. Cover and freeze up to 12 hours, if desired; let stand at room temperature 15 to 20 minutes before serving. Serve with Chocolate-Mint Sauce. Yield: one 10-inch dessert.

Whipped Cream Frosting

3   cups whipping cream
3   tablespoons powdered sugar
1½   teaspoons vanilla extract

Beat whipping cream at low speed with an electric mixer until thickened; add sugar and vanilla, beating until firm peaks form. Yield: 6 cups.

Chocolate-Mint Sauce

¾   cup half-and-half
1   (10-ounce) package mint chocolate morsels
1½   cups miniature marshmallows
¼   teaspoon salt
1   teaspoon vanilla extract

Heat half-and-half in a heavy saucepan over low heat. Stir in chocolate morsels, marshmallows, and salt; cook, stirring constantly, until chocolate and marshmallows melt. Remove from heat, and stir in vanilla. Yield: 1½ cups.

Note: Mama always dipped her knife in hot water to make cutting this cake easier.

Thanks, Mama ...

for teachin' me that dyin' is a part of life. But I sure wish it wasn't.

Alabama Ice Cream Squares

2½   cups vanilla wafer crumbs, divided
4   (1-ounce) squares unsweetened chocolate
1⅓   cups butter or margarine
3   cups sifted powdered sugar
1   cup chopped pecans, toasted
¼   cup water
2   teaspoons vanilla extract
½   gallon butter pecan ice cream (rectangular carton)
Garnishes: chocolate shavings, chocolate-dipped pecan halves

Thanks, Mama …

*for teachin'
me what love is.*

Spread 1 cup vanilla wafer crumbs in bottom of a buttered
13- x 9- x 2-inch dish; set aside.

Combine 4 ounces unsweetened chocolate and butter in
a saucepan; cook over low heat until chocolate melts. Remove
from heat. Add powdered sugar, chopped pecans, water, and
vanilla, stirring until blended. Stir in remaining 1½ cups
vanilla wafer crumbs. Spread mixture over crumbs in dish,
and freeze at least 3 hours.

Cut ice cream crosswise into ½-inch slices; arrange over
chocolate layer, carefully spreading top of ice cream until
smooth. Cover and freeze until firm.

Let dessert stand 5 minutes before serving. Garnish, if
desired. Yield: 12 to 15 servings.

Alabama Ice Cream Squares, page 90

Almond-Macaroon Tart, page 104

"Life is like a box of chocolates"

Pies and Pastries

Once in Vietnam Bubba tol' me 'bout his Mama's "Miss'ippi Mud Pie," on account of Bubba knew I was crazy 'bout chocolate and 'cause him an' me spent so much time in the mud together. Well, I wadn't very fond of mud, so I wadn't sure I would like tastin' mud pie. But when I got back from the war and asked my Mama to make Miss'ippi Mud Pie, it was the best thing I ever put in my mouth. Turns out mud's good.

Chocolate-'Nanner Pie

¼	cup butter or margarine, softened
1	(3-ounce) package cream cheese, softened
1½	cups sifted powdered sugar
¼	cup whipping cream
½	teaspoon vanilla extract
3	bananas, sliced
1	(6-ounce) can pineapple juice
1	baked 9-inch pastry shell
½	cup chopped pecans, toasted
2	(1-ounce) squares semisweet chocolate
1	cup whipping cream
3	tablespoons powdered sugar

Beat butter and cream cheese at medium speed with an electric mixer until creamy; gradually add 1½ cups powdered sugar alternately with ¼ cup whipping cream, beginning and ending with powdered sugar. Stir in vanilla. Set filling aside.

Toss banana slices in pineapple juice; drain. Pat slices dry with paper towels. Spoon half of filling into baked pastry shell. Arrange banana slices over filling. Top with remaining filling, and sprinkle with pecans. Set pie aside.

Melt 2 squares semisweet chocolate in a heavy saucepan over low heat. Spoon into a small heavy-duty, zip-top plastic bag. Snip a tiny hole in 1 corner of bag, using scissors; drizzle over pecans and filling. Set aside.

Beat 1 cup whipping cream at low speed with electric mixer until foamy; gradually add 3 tablespoons powdered sugar, beating until soft peaks form. Spoon whipped cream into a large heavy-duty, zip-top plastic bag. Snip a ½-inch hole in 1 corner of bag, using scissors. Pipe dollops around outside edge. Yield: one 9-inch pie.

Chocolate-Cream Cheese Pie

1   (8-ounce) package cream cheese, softened
¾   cup sifted powdered sugar
¼   cup cocoa
1   (8-ounce) container frozen whipped topping, thawed
1   (6-ounce) chocolate-flavored crumb crust
½   cup coarsely chopped pecans

Combine first 3 ingredients in a large mixing bowl; beat at medium speed with an electric mixer until soft and creamy. Add whipped topping, folding until smooth. Spread over crumb crust, and sprinkle with pecans. Serve immediately, or store in refrigerator. Yield: one 9-inch pie.

Thanks, Mama …

for helpin' me understand that Bubba will always be my very best good friend— even in heaven.

Bayou La Batre Meringue Pie

1¾   cups sugar, divided
⅓   cup all-purpose flour
¼   cup cocoa
2   cups milk
4   large eggs, separated
2   tablespoons butter or margarine, melted and cooled
1   baked 9-inch pastry shell
½   teaspoon cream of tartar

Thanks, Mama ...

for Sunday dinners of fried chicken an' chocolate pie with meringue piled up to heaven.

Combine 1¼ cups sugar, flour, and cocoa in a heavy saucepan. Combine milk, egg yolks, and melted butter; beat, using a wire whisk, until mixture is well blended. Gradually add milk mixture to sugar mixture, stirring until smooth.

Cook chocolate mixture over medium heat, stirring constantly, until thickened and bubbly (about 10 minutes). Spoon chocolate mixture into pastry shell; set aside.

Beat egg whites and cream of tartar at high speed with an electric mixer until foamy. Gradually add remaining ½ cup sugar, 1 tablespoon at a time, beating until stiff peaks form and sugar dissolves (2 to 4 minutes). Spread meringue mixture over chocolate filling, sealing to edge of pastry. Bake at 325° for 25 minutes or until golden. Yield: one 9-inch pie.

96

Chocolate-Strawberry Truffle Pie

1	(6-ounce) package semisweet chocolate morsels
1	(8-ounce) package cream cheese, cubed
2	tablespoons butter or margarine
¼	cup sifted powdered sugar
3	tablespoons Triple Sec or orange juice
1	baked 9-inch pastry shell
3½	cups fresh strawberries, hulled
¼	cup red currant jelly, melted
½	cup whipping cream
2	tablespoons powdered sugar
½	teaspoon grated orange rind

Garnishes: orange rind strips, mint leaves

Combine first 3 ingredients in top of a double boiler; place over boiling water. Cook, stirring constantly, until melted. Remove from heat, and stir in ¼ cup powdered sugar and Triple Sec. Spread mixture evenly into pastry shell. Cool.

Place strawberries, stem side down, over chocolate mixture; brush with jelly. Refrigerate 2 to 3 hours.

Combine whipping cream and 2 tablespoons powdered sugar in a small mixing bowl, and beat until soft peaks form. Fold in grated orange rind. Top each serving with a dollop of whipped cream mixture. Garnish, if desired. Yield: one 9-inch pie.

German Chocolate Pie

1	(4-ounce) package sweet baking chocolate
¼	cup butter or margarine
1	(13-ounce) can evaporated milk
1½	cups sugar
3	tablespoons cornstarch
⅛	teaspoon salt
2	large eggs
1	teaspoon vanilla extract
2	unbaked 8-inch pastry shells
1⅓	cups flaked coconut
½	cup chopped pecans

Garnishes: whipped cream, chocolate shavings

Combine chocolate and butter in a saucepan; cook over low heat, stirring until chocolate melts. Remove from heat, and gradually stir in milk; set aside.

Combine sugar, cornstarch, and salt in a bowl; add eggs and vanilla, mixing well. Gradually stir in chocolate mixture, using a wire whisk. Pour into pastry shells, and sprinkle with coconut and pecans. Bake at 375° for 45 minutes. (Pie may appear soft, but will become firm after cooling.) Cool at least 4 hours before slicing. Garnish, if desired. Yield: two 8-inch pies.

Groovy Grasshopper Pie

1¼   cups chocolate wafer crumbs (about 32 wafers)
⅓   cup butter or margarine, melted
1   (6-ounce) package chocolate-covered mint wafer
        candies
4   cups miniature marshmallows
¼   cup sugar
2   tablespoons butter or margarine
⅓   cup green crème de menthe
1½   cups whipping cream, whipped

Thanks, Mama ...

*for listenin' to me
when life seemed
real tough.*

Combine chocolate wafer crumbs and melted butter; stir well.
Press crumb mixture evenly into bottom and up sides of a
greased 9-inch pieplate. Bake at 350° for 6 to 8 minutes. Let
cool completely.

Cut 3 mint candies diagonally in half; set aside. Reserve
10 whole candies for garnish. Chop remaining candies; set
aside.

Combine marshmallows, sugar, and 2 tablespoons
butter in top of a double broiler. Bring water to a boil.
Reduce heat to low; cook until marshmallows melt, stirring
frequently. Remove from heat. Stir in crème de menthe. Let
mixture cool to room temperature. Fold in chopped mint
candies and whipped cream. Spread mixture evenly into
prepared crust. Arrange reserved candy halves in center of
pie; cover and freeze until firm.

Pull a vegetable peeler down sides of reserved whole
candies to make tiny shavings. Garnish pie with candy
shavings. Yield: one 9-inch pie.

Bubba's Ice Cream Sundae Pie

2	cups chocolate cookie crumbs
2	cups chopped pecans, toasted and divided
½	cup sugar
½	cup butter or margarine, melted
½	gallon vanilla ice cream, slightly softened
1	cup flaked coconut
1	(11.75-ounce) jar chocolate sauce, divided
2	ripe bananas, sliced
1	cup whipping cream, whipped

Thanks, Mama ...

*for admirin'
almost everything
I ever did.*

Combine cookie crumbs, 1 cup pecans, sugar, and butter. Reserve ¼ cup mixture. Press remaining crumb mixture into bottom of a 9-inch springform pan; set aside.

Cut ice cream in half. Return 1 portion to freezer; cut remaining portion into slices, and arrange evenly (cutting to fit) over crumb crust. Sprinkle coconut and remaining 1 cup pecans over ice cream; drizzle with half of chocolate sauce. Freeze until firm.

Cut remaining portion of ice cream into slices. Arrange over chocolate sauce; top with bananas, and drizzle with remaining chocolate sauce. Top with whipped cream; sprinkle with reserved crumb mixture. Freeze until firm. Cover and return to freezer.

Remove pie from freezer 20 minutes before serving. Yield: 10 to 12 servings.

Note: For chocolate cookie crumbs, Mama always used Oreo brand crumbs, available in a 15-ounce box where baking ingredients are sold.

Mama Blue's Mississippi Mud Pie

3   (1-ounce) squares unsweetened chocolate
1½   cups sifted powdered sugar
½   cup whipping cream
⅓   cup butter or margarine
3   tablespoons light corn syrup
Dash of salt
1   tablespoon vanilla extract
1   (9-inch) graham cracker crust
1   cup chopped pecans, divided
3   cups coffee ice cream, softened and divided
Sweetened whipped cream

Melt chocolate in a heavy saucepan over low heat; add powdered sugar and next 4 ingredients. Cook, stirring constantly, until mixture is smooth. Remove from heat; stir in vanilla, and let cool.

Spread ½ cup chocolate sauce in graham cracker crust; sprinkle with ¼ cup pecans. Freeze 10 minutes. Remove from freezer, and spread 1 cup ice cream over pecans; freeze 20 minutes. Repeat layers twice.

Cover pie, and freeze at least 8 hours. Drizzle remaining chocolate sauce over pie. Pipe whipped cream onto pie, and sprinkle with remaining pecans. Yield: one 9-inch pie.

Turtle Ice Cream Pie

3   cups chocolate wafer crumbs
½   cup butter or margarine, melted
1¼   cups semisweet chocolate morsels
1   cup evaporated milk
1   cup miniature marshmallows
⅛   teaspoon salt
1   quart vanilla ice cream, divided
1   cup pecan halves, toasted

Combine chocolate crumbs and butter; firmly press into a 9-inch deep-dish pieplate, and freeze 15 minutes.

Combine chocolate morsels and next 3 ingredients in a heavy saucepan. Cook over low heat, stirring constantly, until thickened and smooth. Remove from heat, and set aside.

Spread 2 cups ice cream into prepared pieplate; cover and freeze 30 minutes. Pour half of chocolate mixture over ice cream layer; cover and freeze 30 minutes. Spread remaining ice cream over chocolate mixture; cover and freeze 30 minutes. Spread remaining chocolate mixture over ice cream, and top with pecans. Cover and freeze. Yield: one 9-inch pie.

Caramel Turtle Truffle Tart

1⅓   cups all-purpose flour
⅓   cup sugar
½   cup butter, cut into slices
1   large egg
1   teaspoon vanilla extract
1½   cups semisweet chocolate morsels
¾   cup whipping cream, divided
1   (14-ounce) package caramels, unwrapped
3   cups chopped pecans

Thanks, Mama ...

for makin' me realize that God is mysterious an' doesn't always do what we ask him to do.

Position knife blade in food processor bowl; add first 3 ingredients. Process 1 minute or until mixture is crumbly. Remove food pusher. Add egg and vanilla through chute with processor running; process until mixture forms a smooth dough. Press into bottom and up sides of an 11-inch tart pan; prick bottom generously with a fork. Bake at 400° for 10 minutes or until golden; cool. Set aside.

Combine chocolate morsels and ¼ cup whipping cream in a small microwave-safe bowl; microwave on HIGH 1 to 1½ minutes or until chocolate melts, stirring once. Spread 1 cup mixture evenly in bottom of baked pastry, reserving remaining mixture at room temperature. Chill pastry 30 minutes.

Combine caramels and remaining ½ cup whipping cream in a heavy saucepan; cook over low heat, stirring constantly, until caramels melt and mixture is smooth. Stir in pecans, and spread evenly over chocolate layer. Spoon reserved chocolate mixture into a small heavy-duty, zip-top plastic bag. (If chocolate is firm, microwave on HIGH 30 seconds or until soft.) Snip a small hole in 1 corner of bag, using scissors; drizzle chocolate over tart. Chill at least 1 hour. Let stand 30 minutes before serving. Yield: one 11-inch tart.

Almond-Macaroon Tart

Thanks, Mama ...

for teachin'
me to dream.

1¼   cups chocolate wafer crumbs (about 32 wafers)
1   cup sliced blanched almonds, ground
¼   cup butter or margarine, melted
2   egg whites
⅓   cup sugar
1   (7-ounce) package flaked coconut
1   teaspoon vanilla extract
⅓   cup sweetened condensed milk
¼   cup butter or margarine
3   (1-ounce) squares unsweetened chocolate,
      chopped
3   large eggs
½   cup sugar
⅛   teaspoon salt
1   teaspoon vanilla extract
¾   cup whole natural almonds
4   (1-ounce) squares semisweet chocolate, chopped
½   cup whipping cream
1   tablespoon light corn syrup
6   (1-ounce) squares semisweet chocolate, chopped
1   ounce white chocolate, chopped
1½   teaspoons shortening

Combine first 3 ingredients, stirring well. Pat mixture onto bottom and up sides of a lightly greased 11-inch tart pan. Bake at 350° for 10 minutes.

Beat egg whites at high speed with an electric mixer until soft peaks form. Gradually add ⅓ cup sugar, beating 4 minutes or until thick. Stir in coconut, 1 teaspoon vanilla, and condensed milk. Spread coconut mixture over prepared crust.

Melt ¼ cup butter and unsweetened chocolate in a heavy saucepan over medium-low heat. Remove from heat.

Beat 3 eggs at medium speed until thick and pale. Gradually add ½ cup sugar, salt, and 1 teaspoon vanilla, beating until blended. Stir in melted chocolate mixture. Spoon over coconut mixture in pan. Bake at 350° for 40 minutes. Let cool completely; carefully remove sides of tart pan.

Roast whole almonds on a baking sheet at 350° for 8 to 12 minutes. Let cool.

Melt 4 ounces semisweet chocolate in top of a double boiler over hot, not simmering, water. Remove from heat, and let cool until chocolate temperature reaches 90° on an instant read thermometer. Add roasted almonds; stir constantly 2 to 3 minutes or until chocolate begins to set. Remove chocolate-coated almonds, and let dry separately on wax paper.

Bring whipping cream and corn syrup to a boil in a small saucepan. Remove from heat, and pour over 6 ounces semisweet chocolate in a bowl. Let stand 1 minute. Whisk until smooth. Pour chocolate mixture over baked tart. Place chocolate-coated almonds around edge of tart.

Melt white chocolate and shortening in top of double boiler over hot, not simmering, water. Remove from heat, and drizzle over tart. Let stand until topping is set. Yield: one 11-inch tart.

Chocolate Chess Tarts

1   (5-ounce) can evaporated milk
2   (1-ounce) squares unsweetened chocolate
¼   cup butter or margarine
2   large eggs
1¼ cups sugar
1   teaspoon vanilla extract
12 unbaked (3-inch) tart shells

Thanks, Mama ...

*most of all,
for bein' the best
mama in the whole
wide world.*

Combine first 3 ingredients in a small saucepan; cook over low heat, stirring frequently, until chocolate and butter melt. Cool slightly. Combine eggs and sugar in a large bowl; add chocolate mixture and vanilla, stirring until blended. Pour into tart shells; place filled tarts on a baking sheet. Bake at 350° for 30 minutes or until set. Cool on a wire rack. Yield: 1 dozen.

METRIC MEASURE CONVERSIONS

When You Know...	Multiply by... Mass (weight)	To Find Approximate...	Symbol
ounces	28	grams	g
pounds	0.45	kilograms	kg
	(volume)		
teaspoons	5	milliliters	ml
tablespoons	15	milliliters	ml
fluid ounces	30	milliliters	ml
cups	0.24	liters	l
pints	0.47	liters	l
quarts	0.95	liters	l
gallons	3.8	liters	l

METRIC MEASURE EQUIVALENTS

Cup Measure	Volume (Liquid)	Solid (Butter)	Fine Powder (Flour)	Granular (Sugar)	Grain (Rice)
1	250 ml	200 g	140 g	190 g	150 g
¾	188 ml	150 g	105 g	143 g	113 g
⅔	167 ml	133 g	93 g	127 g	100 g
½	125 ml	100 g	70 g	95 g	75 g
⅓	83 ml	67 g	47 g	63 g	50 g
¼	63 ml	50 g	35 g	48 g	38 g
⅛	31 ml	25 g	18 g	24 g	19 g

Index

chocolate chip fudge, c
German chocolate ches
sundaes, chocolate po
pie, chocolate cheeseca
chocolate-mint cookie
chocolate roulage, cho
oatmeal-chocolate chip
mud pie, chocolate tor
hazelnut-toffee cookie
chocolate surprise coo